The Planets

Written by
Cynthia Pratt Nicolson

Illustrated by
Bill Slavin

Kids Can Press

For Sara, Ian and Vanessa

Acknowledgments

I would like to thank Jaymie Matthews of the University of British Columbia for reading over the rough draft of this book and patiently answering my many questions. Also, thanks to Ivan Semeniuk of the Ontario Science Centre for his expert advice and to Martin Hecht of the Lowell Observatory for details on the discovery and naming of Pluto.

My teaching colleagues at Bowen Island Community School are a great help when I am searching for the best way to explain a topic, and my students are excellent "guinea pigs" for the activities. I am grateful to Janice Cashin for her comments on planet rotation and to Brad Daudlin for his help with computers. Thanks to my editor, Val Wyatt, for cheerfully demanding the utmost clarity, and to illustrator Bill Slavin for adding so much humor to the book. Finally, I would like to thank my husband, Donald, for his enthusiastic support.

We acknowledge the support of the Canada Council for the Arts and the Ontario Arts Council for our publishing program.

Published in Canada by:
Kids Can Press Ltd.
29 Birch Avenue
Toronto, Ontario, Canada
M4V 1E2

Published in the U.S. by:
Kids Can Press Ltd.
85 River Rock Drive, Suite 202
Buffalo, NY 14207

Edited by Valerie Wyatt
Text design by Marie Bartholomew
Page layout and cover design by Esperança Melo

Photo credits
All photos used courtesy of NASA.

Printed in Hong Kong by Wing King Tong Co. Ltd.

CM 98 0 9 8 7 6 5 4 3 2 1

Canadian Cataloguing in Publication Data

Nicolson, Cynthia Pratt
　　The planets

(Starting with space)
Includes index.
ISBN 1-55074-512-3

1. Planets – Juvenile literature. I. Slavin, Bill.
II. Title. III. Series.

QB602.N52 1998　　　j523.4　　　C97-932196-4

Contents

Planets around the Sun

Imagine living without TV, videos and electric lights.
What would you do on dark nights?
People long ago watched the stars. They noticed a few
strange dots of light that moved through the stars.
They called these moving lights planets, a word that
means wanderers.

Planet tales

Long ago, people thought the sky was full of magic. They believed that the motions of the planets changed what happened here on Earth.

Early Tahitians worried when Venus and Jupiter were close together in the sky. "The planets are threatening each other," they said. "That means two of our chiefs will soon go to war."

If you see a word you don't know, look it up in the glossary on page 39.

An ancient Chinese poem says the planet Mars landed on Earth in the shape of a young boy. He told the people all about the future, then flew back up into the sky.

The Pawnee people of North America watched the planets cross the wide open skies and said, "If people die of sickness, the planets will take care of their souls."

What is a planet?

A planet is a large object that travels around a star. Earth is a planet. It circles the star we call the Sun. Eight other planets – Mercury, Venus, Mars, Jupiter, Saturn, Uranus, Neptune and Pluto – also circle the Sun. Scientists do not know if there are other planets around distant stars.

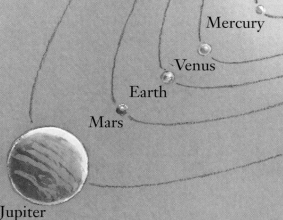

Sun

Mercury

Venus

Earth

Mars

Jupiter

Saturn

Uranus

Neptune

Pluto

What is the solar system?

The solar system is made up of the Sun and the objects circling it. In the solar system, there are 9 planets and more than 60 moons. Thousands of small, rocky lumps called asteroids also circle the Sun. Most of them are between Mars and Jupiter. Far beyond the orbits of the planets is a swarm of icy comets. Their orbits sometimes take them close to the Sun, where they are visible from Earth.

6

How do planets move?

The planets travel around the Sun in almost circular paths called orbits. The Sun's pulling force — gravity — keeps them from flying off into space.

Each planet also rotates around an imaginary axis. Most planets spin with their axes pointing nearly up and down. But Uranus spins on its side.

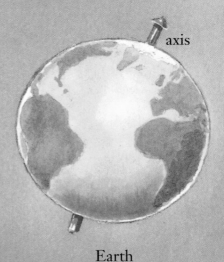

axis

Earth

Why do planets shine?

Planets shine when the Sun's light bounces off them. Unlike stars, they don't glow with their own heat.

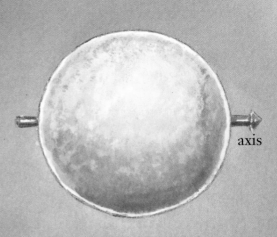

axis

Uranus

How did the solar system begin?

Scientists believe that the solar system took shape from an enormous swirling cloud of gas and dust particles. In the center of the cloud, particles clumped together and formed a new star, the Sun.

Other particles continued to flow like a whirlpool around the Sun. About 4½ billion years ago, the cloud separated into many smaller lumps. They became the planets, moons, asteroids and comets of the solar system.

How big is the solar system?

The solar system is enormous. If you could fly in a jet plane outward from the Sun, it would take you 18 years to reach the Earth. Eight years later, you would pass Mars. Arriving at Jupiter would take another 66 years. And flying past Pluto would take a whopping 700 years.

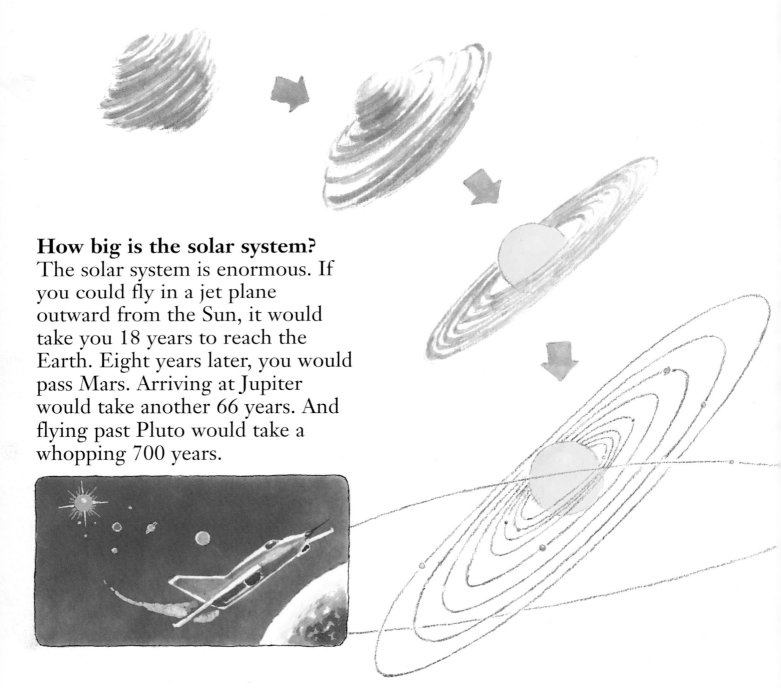

TRY IT!

Make a solar system you can eat

You'll need:
- a large honeydew or small watermelon
- a cantaloupe
- 2 large round apples
- 2 cherries
- a small raspberry
- a pea
- a peppercorn

If the planets were the sizes of the foods shown here, the Sun would be as big as a passenger van. And the distances between planets would be enormous. For example, Pluto would be 9 km (5 ½ mi.) away from Mercury.

Neptune

Uranus

Mars

Saturn

Earth

Mercury

Venus

Pluto

Jupiter

Can you put the foods in the order of planets in the solar system?

Mercury: Racing round the Sun

If you've ever stood near a hot fire on a cold night, you have some idea how Mercury feels. The side facing the Sun sizzles while the side facing away freezes.

Mercury has tall mountains, steep cliffs and broad, flat plains. The plains probably formed long ago, when lava from inside the planet flooded its surface.

What would it be like to visit Mercury?

As you zoom in on Mercury, you might think you are landing on the Moon. Like the Moon, Mercury is spotted with craters formed when asteroids and meteoroids crashed into it.

Mercury has hardly any air, so you'd need oxygen tanks to breathe. You'd also need a special suit to protect you from the extreme cold and heat. Even with all the heavy gear, you'd be able to leap farther and jump higher than on Earth. Mercury's low gravity means you weigh about one-third of your Earth weight.

Why is Mercury so hot – and cold?

Mercury is close to the Sun, so it gets more intense heat than Earth does. On the side facing the sun it is HOT. But it has no blanket of air to keep heat in. So on the side facing away from the sun, it is COLD.

Mercury's temperature changes are the greatest of any planet.

What's inside Mercury?

Inside its rocky outer crust, Mercury has a large core of iron. Because Mercury's core is so big for its size, some scientists think Mercury may once have been much bigger. How did it shrink? A collision with a giant asteroid may have knocked off much of its outer layer.

MERCURY FACTS

Mercury rotates on its axis once every 58 days and 14 hours.

Mercury orbits the Sun in just 88 days, compared with Earth's 365.2 days. Because of the planet's speed, early Roman sky watchers named it after Mercury, the messenger god who sped through the sky on winged feet.

Mercury is the closest planet to the Sun.

Mercury is only a little bigger than our moon.

Craters on Mercury are named after famous composers, authors and artists such as Beethoven, Vivaldi, Dickens and Renoir.

Venus: Sky dazzler

Have you ever wished upon a star? Chances are it wasn't a star at all. Often, the first bright light in the evening sky is Venus, the closest planet to Earth.

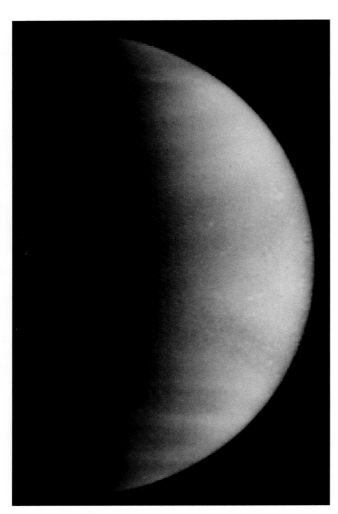

This picture of Venus was taken by the Hubble Space Telescope. The thick clouds that blanket Venus make it difficult to photograph the surface.

What would it be like to visit Venus?

Watch out for lightning as you descend through the yellow clouds of Venus. But don't worry about rain – water evaporates instantly in the heat. On Venus's dry, rocky surface, the temperature reaches 460° C (860° F). That's hot enough to melt lead – and your spaceship.

Need more reasons to avoid Venus? Its atmosphere is poisonous. And the planet's air pressure would crush you instantly. It's 90 times stronger than air pressure on Earth.

The atmosphere of Venus traps the Sun's heat, making it the hottest planet in the solar system.

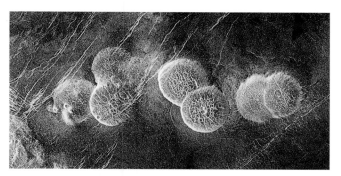

These domes on Venus formed when lava spurted out of volcanoes. Scientists aren't sure if Venus's volcanoes are still active.

Why does Venus look so bright?

Venus is completely covered in a thick blanket of yellowish clouds. These clouds reflect sunlight, making the planet shine in the evening or early morning sky.

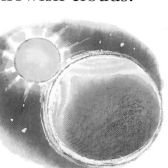

VENUS FACTS

A year on Venus is 224.7 days long. That's how long it takes Venus to orbit the Sun.

Venus rotates on its axis once every 243 days and 5 hours.

Venus has no moons.

Venus is sometimes called Earth's twin because it is almost the same size as Earth.

Venus looks so beautiful that people wanted to give it a beautiful name. They called it Venus, after the Roman goddess of love.

Earth rotates from west to east. Venus rotates in the opposite direction.

Almost all the land forms on Venus are named after women, such as the Greek goddess Aphrodite and the pilot Amelia Earhart.

Earth: Our blue home

**Did you take a really long trip last year? Of course, you did.
In one year, you flew all the way around the Sun.
Your spaceship? Our very own planet Earth.**

This photo of Earth was taken by the *Apollo 17* astronauts as they traveled toward the Moon.

Why is Earth a good place to live?
Earth is the only planet we know of where people, plants and animals can survive. It has the oxygen and water we need and the right temperature for living things. If Earth were closer to the Sun, it would be much too hot. Farther away, it would be too cold.

Summer sunlight hits Town X directly.

Winter sunlight hits Town X at an angle.

Earth's tilt gives us seasons. Summer days are long and hot. Winter days are short and cold.

What's inside Earth?
Under Earth's crust are layers of rock and metal.

The crust is like a thin skin of hard rock.

The mantle contains rock so hot that it is slightly soft, like modeling clay.

Like a cracked eggshell, Earth's crust and upper mantle are divided into huge pieces.

The outer core contains hot liquid metal.

The inner core is solid metal.

EARTH FACTS

Earth orbits the Sun in 365.2 days (one year).

Earth rotates on its axis in 23 hours and 56 minutes (one day).

Earth is the fifth largest planet in the solar system.

Earth has one moon, which revolves around the planet every 27.3 days (about one month).

It takes about eight minutes for sunlight to travel from the Sun to Earth.

5

Mars: A red mystery

Is there life on Mars? People have asked that question for centuries. They've imagined bug-eyed Martians with dangling tentacles. But recent clues point to a strange new story of Martian life.

Mars is a cold place. Its polar ice caps (shown in white) are made of ice and frozen carbon dioxide, sometimes called dry ice.

Mars looks reddish because of rust in its iron-rich soil. This color reminded people of anger and blood, so they named the planet after the Roman god of war.

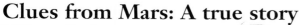

Clues from Mars: A true story

When Roberta Score picked up a rock in Antarctica in 1984, she didn't know she was holding a piece of Mars.

The greenish, potato-size rock was sent to NASA's Johnson Space Center in Texas. There, it was stored for ten years. Then scientists began to check it out.

Inside the rock they found air bubbles that matched Martian air samples. They also discovered minerals that are sometimes produced by living things.

Powerful microscopes revealed tiny tubelike structures, each far thinner than a human hair. Were these fossils of ancient creatures?

In 1996, NASA scientists announced that the rock was formed on Mars about 4 1/2 billion years ago. It was thrown into space when an asteroid or comet crashed into the planet. After circling the Sun for 15 million years, the Martian meteorite landed on Earth.

The meteorite may show that life once existed on Mars. But scientists want more proof. New space probes will collect more samples. And scientists will continue to test Roberta Score's rock.

The Martian meteorite found in Antarctica.

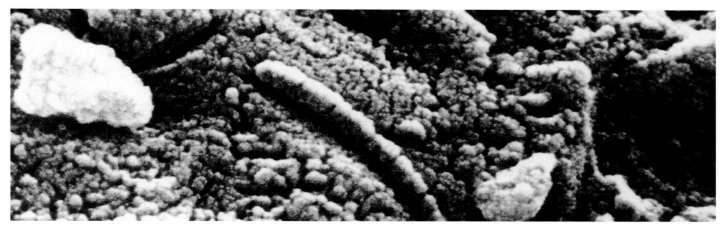

The tubelike forms inside the meteorite may be fossils of living things.

What would it be like to visit Mars?

Admire the peach-colored sky as you descend toward Mars. But don't be tempted to step out onto the rust-colored soil. The atmosphere is so thin you'd be instantly sunburned by the Sun's harmful rays. The low air pressure would make your blood bubble. And Martian air is almost all carbon dioxide, the stuff you breathe out.

This picture from the 1997 Pathfinder mission shows the Sojourner rover on the rocky surface of Mars. The large rock was named Yogi.

MARS FACTS

A Martian year is 687 Earth days long. That's how long it takes Mars to orbit the Sun.

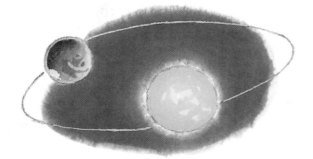

Mars rotates on its axis once every 24 hours and 37 minutes, so a Martian day is almost the same length as an Earth day.

Because Mars is tilted like the Earth, it has seasons.

Mars has two small, potato-shaped moons, named Phobos and Deimos. These Greek words mean "fear" and "panic."

Mars is about half the size of Earth.

Olympus Mons on Mars is the highest known mountain in the solar system. This volcano is three times taller than Mount Everest.

TRY IT!
Test for signs of life

You'll need:
- 3 tall drinking glasses labeled 1, 2 and 3
- 250 mL (1 c.) cornmeal
- 15 mL (1 tbsp.) baking soda
- 15 mL (1 tbsp.) yeast
- 125 mL (¹/₂ c.) sugar
- 500 mL (2 c.) warm water
- a spoon

1. Divide the cornmeal among the three glasses. Add the baking soda to glass 2. Add the yeast to glass 3.

2. Dissolve the sugar in the warm water.

3. Pour one-third of the sugar and water solution into each glass. Stir gently. Check the glasses after 1 minute, 10 minutes and again after 20 minutes. What do you see?

No reaction, means no life. A quick fizzing shows an ordinary chemical reaction — still no life. But a reaction that starts slowly and lasts a long time means you've found something alive and growing.

In 1976, a space probe did similar tests on soil samples from Mars. Scientists were looking for a long, slow reaction. The space probe tests showed no signs of life. What did *your* test find? See page 39.

6

Jupiter: A gas giant

If you wanted to land a spaceship on Jupiter, you'd have a major problem. Why? There's no land to land on!

What would it be like to visit Jupiter?

Jupiter doesn't have a solid surface like Earth. Instead, it's made of thick gases. Visiting Jupiter would be like trying to land on a cloud.

The pull of gravity at Jupiter's surface is 2 1/2 times stronger than on Earth, so you would quickly be pulled deeper into the planet. Scientists think Jupiter might have a small, solid inner core wrapped in an ocean of liquid hydrogen and helium. But you'd be crushed and cooked by the immense pressure and heat of Jupiter's inner layers before you reached the core.

The Great Red Spot is a hurricane that has raged on Jupiter for at least 300 years. It is so huge that three Earths could fit inside it.

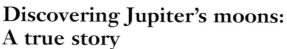

Discovering Jupiter's moons: A true story

In 1609, in northern Italy, a math professor by the name of Galileo Galilei heard news of a marvelous invention. By mounting two lenses inside a tube, you could see distant objects as if they were nearby.

Galileo quickly constructed a telescope for himself. On January 7, 1610, he aimed his 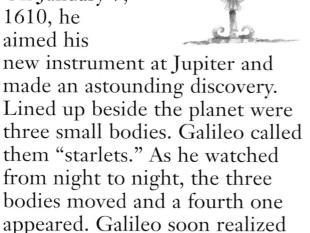 new instrument at Jupiter and made an astounding discovery. Lined up beside the planet were three small bodies. Galileo called them "starlets." As he watched from night to night, the three bodies moved and a fourth one appeared. Galileo soon realized that he was watching four moons revolving around Jupiter.

At the time, most people believed Earth was the center of the universe. Now Galileo had proof that some things did *not* revolve around Earth. If moons circled Jupiter, he argued, was it not possible that all the planets, including Earth, revolve around the Sun?

Galileo's ideas so shocked people that he was locked up for the last nine years of his life. Even so, Galileo's ideas changed astronomy forever. Nearly 400 years later, a space probe began taking close-up photos of Jupiter and its moons. The name of the probe? *Galileo*.

Jupiter with four of its sixteen moons: Io, Europa, Ganymede and Callisto. Ganymede is the biggest moon in the solar system.

Why does Jupiter look striped?

Jupiter's stripes are bands of pink, red, yellow, tan and white clouds. The lightest bands are called zones. They are made of ice crystals of ammonia. Darker bands, called belts, contain traces of other chemicals. Strong winds and Jupiter's rapid spin stretch the clouds into stripes.

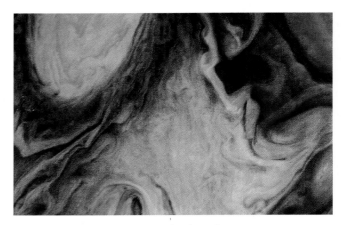

Jupiter's multicolored clouds.

JUPITER FACTS

A Jupiter year is about 11.9 Earth years long. That's how long it takes Jupiter to orbit the Sun.

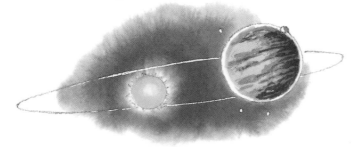

If Jupiter were hollow, all the other planets would fit inside it.

Jupiter rotates on its axis once every 9 hours and 50 minutes.

Because it was so big and bright in the sky, early Romans named Jupiter after their chief god.

TRY IT!
Make a model of Jupiter's stormy surface

You'll need:
- 150 mL (²/₃ c.) milk
- a large pie plate
- red and yellow food coloring
- liquid dish detergent

1. Pour the milk into the pie plate.

2. Gently add two drops of red food coloring to one half of the milk.

3. Add two drops of yellow food coloring to the other half.

4. Carefully drop detergent into the center of each spot of food coloring.

5. Spin the plate gently two or three times to mix the colors. Watch the swirling bands and pretend you are in a spaceship approaching Jupiter.

7

Saturn: Rings of wonder

If you had to pick the most beautiful planet, which would it be? What about Saturn with its multicolored rings?

What would it be like to visit Saturn?

The view as you approach the planet would be spectacular. No other planet has such a broad and colorful system of rings.

You could hover a while in Saturn's cold upper clouds, but don't descend. Like Jupiter, Saturn is made mostly of hydrogen and helium gases, so your spaceship would have nowhere to touch down. Saturn becomes hotter and denser toward its center. Get too close and you might be squished and roasted.

SATURN FACTS

A year on Saturn is 29.5 Earth years long. That's how long it takes Saturn to orbit the Sun.

Saturn is the second largest planet in the solar system, after Jupiter.

Jupiter   Saturn

Saturn is not as dense as Earth. If you could find a swimming pool big enough, Saturn would float.

Scientists believe Saturn might have a liquid interior and small, rocky core.

Saturn rotates on its axis once every 10 hours and 14 minutes.

Except at its poles, all the winds on Saturn blow in one direction – east.

Because Saturn moves slowly and steadily across the sky, early people said it was like an old man. Ancient Romans called the planet Saturn after the old father of Jupiter.

Why does Saturn have rings?

Saturn's rings may have formed when a small moon drifted too close to the planet and was ripped to pieces. Bits of dust and ice, from the size of a pea to the size of a house, spread around the planet in thousands of separate rings.

Saturn's ring system is about 1 km (⁵/₈ mi.) thick.

Does Saturn have moons?

Saturn has 18 named moons, plus a few smaller moons that haven't yet been named. The major moons are outside Saturn's rings.

Titan, the largest moon, is bigger than the planet Mercury. It is the only moon known to have a dense atmosphere. Enceladus is covered with smooth ice, making it the shiniest body in the solar system. Iapetus is white on one side and black on the other.

Saturn with its moons Dione, Tethys, Mimas, Enceladus, Rhea and Titan.

TRY IT!
Pace through space

To measure vast distances in space, scientists sometimes use Astronomical Units (AU). One AU is the distance from the Sun to Earth — 150 million km (93 million mi.). In this activity, you'll make your own foot equal to one AU and step to the edge of the solar system.

You'll need:
- a marking pen
- 10 paper cups

1. Label the cups Sun, Mercury, Venus, Earth, Mars, Jupiter, Saturn, Uranus, Neptune and Pluto.

2. Set the Sun cup at one end of a sidewalk or school hallway.

3. Place your heel against the Sun cup. Set Mercury by your instep, Venus by the joint of your big toe and Earth by the tip of your big toe.

4. Continue to take steps by placing the heel of one foot against the toe of the other. Set your remaining cups at these distances from the Sun:

Mars - 1 ¹/₂ steps
Jupiter - 5 steps
Saturn - 9 ¹/₂ steps
Uranus - 19 steps
Neptune - 30 steps
Pluto - 40 steps

These are the average distances of the planets from the Sun. Pluto's long, oval orbit sometimes brings it closer to the Sun than Neptune.

Uranus: Rolling along

The giant planet Uranus rolls along its path around the Sun on its side. Some scientists think something big may have crashed into Uranus and knocked it over.

Uranus with 4 of its 11 rings showing.

What would it be like to visit Uranus?

As you head toward Uranus, watch for its narrow, black rings. They're much harder to see than those of Saturn.

Methane gas in the upper atmosphere gives Uranus a blue-green color. As you descend, your spaceship is surrounded by a cold, unbreathable fog of hydrogen and helium. Fierce winds blow you along at 700 km/h (435 m.p.h.), making landing difficult. But that doesn't matter because there's nowhere to land. Like Jupiter and Saturn, Uranus is a gas planet.

Uranus's narrow rings are made of chunks of black ice.

Does Uranus have moons?

Uranus has 17 moons. Ten of them were discovered by the *Voyager 2* spacecraft in 1986. Titania, the biggest, is about half the size of our moon. Scientists think an asteroid may have shattered the moon Miranda. When the pieces fell back together, the tiny moon looked like a patchwork quilt.

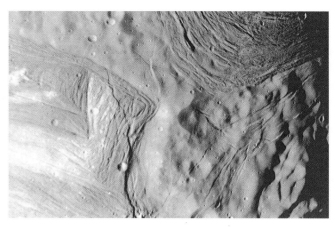

Uranus's moon Miranda with its patchwork surface.

URANUS FACTS

A Uranus year is 84 Earth years long. That's how long it takes Uranus to orbit the Sun.

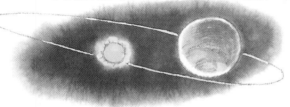

Uranus rotates on its side once every 17 hours and 14 minutes.

Uranus was the first planet to be discovered with a telescope. It was sighted in 1781.

Scientists think that Uranus may have an inner liquid layer, surrounding a rocky core.

Some people wanted to name Uranus after its discoverer, a music teacher named William Herschel. But instead it was named after Uranus, father of Saturn and grandfather of Jupiter in Roman myths.

Neptune: Another blue planet

Neptune looks like a tropical sea, blue and beautiful. But don't bother getting out the beach towels — this planet is anything but tropical.

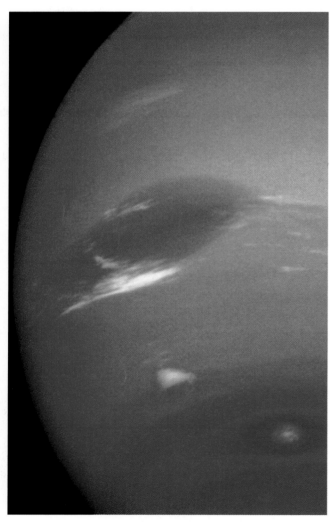

A white cloud scoots around Neptune every 16 hours or so. Scientists call it — what else — "the scooter."

What would it be like to visit Neptune?

Because Neptune is so far from the Sun, it is freezing cold. The temperature in the tops of the clouds is about -175°C (-283°F). And it's windy. Blowing at speeds of up to 1120 km/h (700 m.p.h.), Neptune's winds are the fastest in the solar system.

Like Jupiter, Saturn and Uranus, Neptune is covered in a thick layer of gas. If you could penetrate it, you'd find yourself floating in an ocean of water, ammonia and methane.

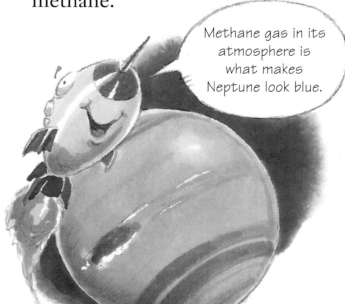

Methane gas in its atmosphere is what makes Neptune look blue.

30

Does Neptune have moons?
Neptune has eight moons. Some are so small that scientists call them moonlets.

Neptune's biggest moon, Triton, is a strange place. It's the coldest body in the solar system and has a cracked, icy surface that looks like the skin of a cantaloupe. Its polar ice cap has volcanoes that erupt, spewing gas and dust 8 km (5 mi.) into the sky.

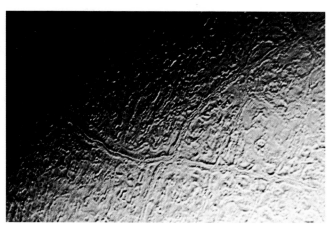

Is this a cantaloupe or is it Neptune's moon Triton? You're right if you guessed Triton.

NEPTUNE FACTS

A Neptune year is 164.8 Earth years long. That's how long it takes Neptune to orbit the Sun.

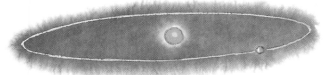

Neptune rotates on its axis once every 16 hours and 7 minutes.

Neptune has four rings. Unlike the chunky rings of Uranus, Neptune's rings are made of tiny particles.

Neptune was named after the Roman god of the sea because it is mostly liquid. Scientists think Neptune also has a small, rocky core.

A space probe has passed closer to Neptune than any other planet. In 1989, *Voyager 2* cruised 4800 km (3000 mi.) above Neptune's cloud tops.

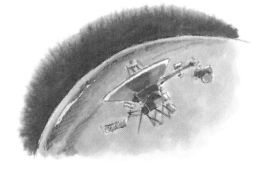

Pluto: The puzzle planet

What would you name a new planet? When the ninth planet was discovered, 11-year-old Venetia Burney thought it should be named Pluto. Pluto was the Greek god of the dead — the perfect name for a dark, gloomy planet. An astronomer friend shared her idea with other astronomers. They agreed. The new planet was officially named Pluto.

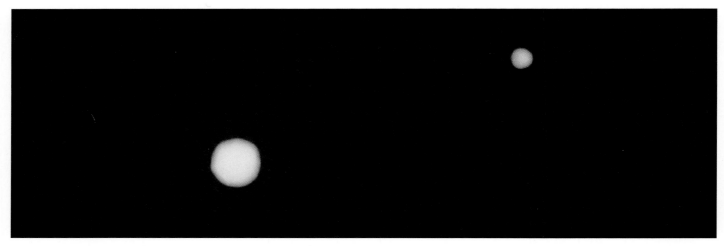

Pluto and its moon, Charon. Because Pluto is so far away, these photos had to be taken with a special Faint Object Camera aboard the Hubble Space Telescope.

What would it be like to visit Pluto?

Don't expect a warm welcome after your long journey to Pluto. Even when the planet is at its closest to the Sun, the temperature is a bone-chilling -233°C (-387°F).

To explore Pluto's icy, rocky surface, you might want to bring along some extra weights. Your weight on Pluto would be $1/20$ of what it is on Earth. Without extra weights, each step would be like a high jump.

PLUTO FACTS

A year on Pluto is 247.7 Earth years. That's how long it takes Pluto to orbit the Sun.

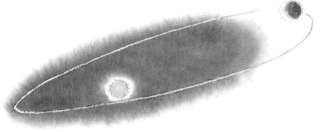

Pluto rotates on its axis once every six days and nine hours.

Pluto is the planet farthest away from the Sun in our solar system. Most of the planets have been visited by a space probe. But not Pluto – it's just too far away.

Pluto's thin atmosphere is made of nitrogen and carbon monoxide.

Pluto was discovered in 1930 by Clyde Tombaugh at the Lowell Observatory in Flagstaff, Arizona. He was looking for a planet whose gravity might be pulling on Uranus and Neptune.

Pluto's orbit is tilted compared to the paths of other planets.

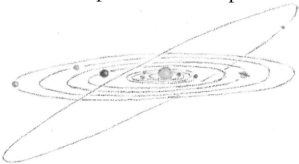

Some scientists think Pluto should be called a "planetesimal" because it's so small. It is smaller than our moon.

Are there any more planets in our solar system?

Some astronomers used to think a tenth planet might have pulled Uranus and Neptune off course around 1900. But evidence from Voyager 2 showed they were wrong. Now most astronomers agree that there are no more planets.

	How far is it from the Sun?	What is its diameter?	How long does it take to rotate on its axis?*	How long does it take to orbit the Sun?	How many moons does it have?	Does it have rings?
MERCURY	58 million km (36 million mi.)	4879 km (3,031 mi.)	58 days 14 hours	88 days	0	no
VENUS	108 million km (67 million mi.)	12 104 km (7,521 mi.)	243 days 5 hours	224.7 days	0	no
EARTH	150 million km (93 million mi.)	12 756 km (7,926 mi.)	23 hours 56 minutes	365.2 days	1	no
MARS	228 million km (142 million mi.)	6794 km (4,217 mi.)	24 hours 37 minutes	687 days	2	no
JUPITER	778 million km (438 million mi.)	142 980 km (88,700 mi.)	9 hours 50 minutes	11.9 years	16	yes
SATURN	1427 million km (886 million mi.)	120 540 km (74,600 mi.)	10 hours 14 minutes	29.5 years	18	yes
URANUS	3 billion km (2 billion mi.)	51 120 km (31,800 mi.)	17 hours 14 minutes	84 years	17	yes
NEPTUNE	4 billion km (3 billion mi.)	49 530 km (30,770 mi.)	16 hours 7 minutes	164.8 years	8	yes
PLUTO	6 billion km (3.5 billion mi.)	2320 km (1,457 mi.)	6 days 9 hours	247.7 years	1	no

* On most planets, rotation time roughly equals one "day," the time from sunrise to sunrise. On Mercury, Venus and Uranus, however, rotation time does not equal a day. From one sunrise to the next on Mercury is 176 Earth days and on Venus, 117 Earth days. Because Uranus spins on its side, some parts of the planet are in darkness for 42 Earth years at a time.

TRY IT!
Match postcards with planets

Al the Alien sent you postcards from his tour of the solar system. Trouble is, Al forgot to tell you which planet was which. Can you figure it out? (Answers on page 39.)

②

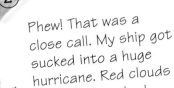

Phew! That was a close call. My ship got sucked into a huge hurricane. Red clouds swirled around — I thought I would never get out alive.

My Earthling Friend
Planet Earth,
Solar System,
Milky Way Galaxy,
The Universe

①

Today I saw a volcano three times higher than Earth's puny Mount Everest. Now I'm back in my spaceship trying to wash all the red dust off my antennae.

My Earthling Friends,
Planet Earth,
Solar System,
Milky Way Galaxy,
The Universe

③

Brrr! I'm freezing! This has got to be the darkest, gloomiest place in the whole solar system. From here, the Sun looks tiny.

My Earthling Frie
Planet Earth,
Solar System,
Milky Way Galaxy,
The Universe

④

Hey — your moon astronauts would feel right at home here. It's got tons of craters and almost no air. Trouble is, while one side of the planet freezes, the other sizzles.

⑤

Choke! Gasp! No way I'm going down through those yellow clouds! My throat is burning and I feel like I've been roasted.

My Earthling Friends,
Planet Earth,
Solar System,
Milky Way Galaxy,
The Universe

⑥

This has got to be one fancy planet. You should see the rings! I mean, I saw thin bands around Jupiter, Neptune and Uranus but these ones beat them all.

My Earthling Frie
Planet Earth,
Solar System,
Milky Way Galaxy,
The Universe

⑦

Today, for the first time, I saw trees. Amazing! I also spotted some birds, tigers, monkeys, flowers and dragonflies. This place is terrific — I hope people take care of it.

My Earthling Friends,
Planet Earth,
Solar System,
Milky Way Galaxy,
The Universe

How do we know about the planets?

For centuries, people learned about the planets by watching them from Earth. Even before telescopes, people could identify Mercury, Venus, Mars, Jupiter and Saturn.

Early telescopes allowed astronomers to spot the moons of Jupiter and the rings of Saturn. More powerful telescopes made for better observations. Telescopes were even put in orbit to escape the blurring of Earth's atmosphere. But the details of the planets were still hard to see.

In the 1960s, scientists began sending space probes into the solar system to get a better look at the planets. These small, robotlike spaceships carry no people. When a probe comes near a planet, it collects images and radar readings of the planet's surface. The information is beamed back to scientists' computers on Earth.

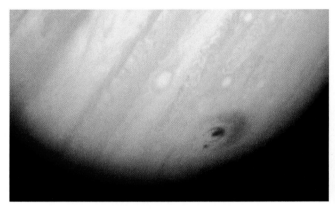

The Hubble Space Telescope took this picture of a comet crashing into Jupiter. The crash site is a red "dimple" on the lower part of the picture.

A space probe passes close to one of Jupiter's moons.

TRY IT!
See some planets for yourself

You don't need a telescope to see Venus, Jupiter, Mars, Mercury and Saturn. Here are some tips on how to find planets in the night sky. Happy hunting!

1. Call a planetarium or look in the latest issue of an astronomy magazine to find out which planets can be seen this month and where they can be found.

2. Without staring directly at the Sun, notice where it crosses the sky during the day. At night, you can find the planets near this same band of sky.

3. Find a viewing place away from bright lights, tall trees and buildings. Use a compass to find north, south, east and west. You'll need to know these directions to find your way around the sky.

Once you've found Jupiter, check it out with binoculars. You should be able to see some of its moons.

One way to tell if something is a planet is that planets don't twinkle like stars do. They shine steadily.

You can usually find Venus by looking east just before sunrise or west just after sunset. The planet looks like an extremely bright star low in the sky.

Why study the planets?

People have always been curious about the planets. Some questions have been answered but many more remain. Scientists are still puzzled about what's inside the giant planets Jupiter, Saturn, Uranus and Neptune. They want to know if Venus has active volcanoes and if there is life on Mars. And they want to see if what has happened on other planets could happen to Earth. Learning about distant worlds helps us understand and take care of our own planet Earth.

Glossary

asteroid: a rocky object orbiting the Sun, much smaller than a planet

astronomer: someone who studies stars, planets and other objects in space

astronomical unit (AU): the average distance from Earth to the Sun, about 150 million km (93 million mi.)

atmosphere: a layer of gases surrounding a planet

axis: an imaginary line around which a planet spins

binoculars: an instrument that helps you see faraway objects more clearly

comet: a ball of ice and dust that orbits the Sun

core: the innermost part of a planet, moon or star

crater: a round hole made by a meteorite, or by a volcano collapsing

crust: the outer covering of a planet or moon

gas: a form of matter made up of tiny particles that are not connected to each other and so can move freely in space. Air is made up of gases.

gravity: an invisible pulling force that holds everything on Earth, keeps the Moon circling Earth and holds Earth and the planets in orbits around the Sun.

hurricane: a violent wind storm

meteorite: a space rock that has crashed into the surface of a planet or moon

moon: a small planet-like body that circles a planet

orbit: the path an object takes through space

oxygen: a gas we need to breathe

planet: a large object that orbits a star and does not make its own light. Earth is a planet that circles a star called the Sun.

rotation: the spinning of a planet on its axis

solar system: the Sun and its planets, moons and smaller orbiting bodies

telescope: an instrument that makes very faraway objects seem nearer. Telescopes are often used to look at planets and moons.

space probe: a robot-like spaceship with no human crew

Answers

Page 19: The yeast in glass 3 is a living organism. It feeds on the sugar and produces bubbles of carbon dioxide gas.

Page 35: 1. Mars, 2. Jupiter, 3. Pluto, 4. Mercury, 5. Venus, 6. Saturn, 7. Earth.

Index

The Missing Ball of String

The Missing Ball of String

By Nancy L. Robison

Drawings by Raymond Burns

GARRARD PUBLISHING COMPANY
CHAMPAIGN, ILLINOIS

Copyright © 1977 by Garrard Publishing Company.   All rights reserved. Manufactured in the U.S.A.
International Standard Book Number: 0-8116-4306-9   Library of Congress Catalog Card Number: 77-8709

The Missing Ball of String

Peter picked up
the ball of string.
He went outside
to fly his kite.

Peter's brother, Tim,
was fixing his bicycle.
"Peter, come help me,"
called Tim.

Peter put his kite
and ball of string
on the table.
He went to help Tim.

When he came back,
the string was gone.
"Where's my string?"
he asked.
Peter looked
under the table.

He looked
around the yard.
"Who took my string?"
he asked.

Peter saw his sister, Kim.
She was reading a book.
"Did you take
my ball of string?"
Peter asked Kim.

"No," she said.
"What would I want
with your old ball of string?"

"Ginger,
where is my ball of string?"
Peter asked.

Ginger opened one eye
and looked at Peter.
"No, you didn't take it,"
he said.
"You're a sleepy old cat."

Peter went into the house
to get some more string.
He found some here.
He found some there.

He found more here.

He found more there.

"What are you doing?" Tim asked.
"I'm looking for more string,"
Peter said.
"My ball of string is missing."
"Don't take that string,"
Tim shouted.

Just then, mother came home.
"Peter, will you get the box
out of the car," mother asked.
"Okay," said Peter.

Peter went outside.
He got the box
from the car.

He took it to mother.
"May I have this string?"
Peter asked his mother.
"I have to make
a new ball of string."

"Where is the string
I gave you?"
asked mother.
"I don't know," said Peter.
"I put it on the table,
and now it's missing."
Just then, father came in.
"What's this about missing string?"
he asked.
"My ball of string was on the table,
and now it's gone," said Peter.
"Oh, you'll find it,"
father said.
"Come and help me."

Peter went to help father.
"Hold the ladder for me,"
father said.
"I'm going to wash these
windows."

"Sure," said Peter.
Peter looked around the yard.
"Where is that missing
ball of string?"
Peter said to himself.

Just then,
Jack came into the yard.
"Hi!" Jack said to Peter.
"What can we do?"

"Let's fly my kite,"
Peter said.
"But first
we have to make
a new string ball."

"Where is your old ball?"
asked Jack.
"I don't know," said Peter.
"It's missing.
But I got some more string
from the house.
It's on the table out back."
"Let's go and make a
new string ball," said Jack.
"Then we can
go to the park
and fly your kite."
The boys ran around the house
to the table.

"Now where is that string?"
shouted Peter.
"I put it right here
on the table.
And now it's gone!"
"Maybe a robber took it,"
said Jack. "Let's look."

The boys looked
all around the yard.

"Here is some
of the missing string,"
called Peter.
"Ginger took it.
She's the robber," he shouted.

"Bad Ginger," said Peter.
"Where did you hide
the rest of my string?"
he asked.

"Here's some more string,"
Jack called.
He brought the string
to Peter.

Just then, mother called,
"Here are some cookies for you."
The boys ran to get the cookies.

"Did you find
your ball of string?"
mother asked.
"No," said Peter.
"I think Ginger took it."

"Ginger wouldn't do that,"
said mother.
"She's too old
to play with string.

I see a piece of string,"
she said.
Peter picked it up.

"There's some string
on the car," said Kim.

"Here's some string,"
called father.
Peter and Jack picked up
the missing pieces of string.

"I still think Ginger
took my string,"
Peter said to Jack.
"How did she get
the string up there?"
Jack asked.

"Maybe Ginger
is not the robber,"
said Peter.
"Then who *is* the robber?"
asked Jack.

"There's some string
in the tree,"
Tim told Peter.
Peter looked up
into the tree.
He shouted, "Jack,
look!
There's all my missing string.
And there's the robber!"

Mother and father came to look.
"The robins
are building their nest,"
said mother.
"That's where
your missing string is,"
father said.

"Maybe she needs more string,"
said Peter.
"Let's give her this."
"I'll get
some more string
for your kite,"
mother said.